Ikigai:
A Journey Into Your Purpose

Dr. Linda Burrs

BALBOA.PRESS
A DIVISION OF HAY HOUSE

Balboa Press books may be ordered through booksellers or by contacting:

Balboa Press
A Division of Hay House
1663 Liberty Drive
Bloomington, IN 47403
www.balboapress.com
844-682-1282

Because of the dynamic nature of the Internet, any web addresses or links contained in
this book may have changed since publication and may no longer be valid. The views
expressed in this work are solely those of the author and do not necessarily reflect the views
of the publisher, and the publisher hereby disclaims any responsibility for them.

The author of this book does not dispense medical advice or prescribe the use of any technique as a form of
treatment for physical, emotional, or medical problems without the advice of a physician, either directly or
indirectly. The intent of the author is only to offer information of a general nature to help you in your quest
for emotional and spiritual well-being. In the event you use any of the information in this book for yourself,
which is your constitutional right, the author and the publisher assume no responsibility for your actions.

Any people depicted in stock imagery provided by Getty Images are models,
and such images are being used for illustrative purposes only.
Certain stock imagery © Getty Images.

ISBN: 979-8-7652-4507-1 (sc)
ISBN: 979-8-7652-4506-4 (e)

Library of Congress Control Number: 2023916354

Print information available on the last page.

Balboa Press rev. date: 11/15/2023

Disclaimers

By purchasing this training course, you hereby acknowledge that you are purchasing educational training and/or materials only. No additional support, training, or act on my part is expressly promised or implied. A separate agreement may be entered into contract separate and apart from this e-learning training module. The *training* and downloadable *training materials* are intended to provide helpful and useful *material* on the subjects addressed in the *training modules*.

Dr. Linda J. Burrs and/or Step Up To Success products (including but not limited to training and coaching materials) are for education and/or illustration purposes only, and are provided with the understanding that we are not engaged in rendering legal or other professional opinions. All content and courses presented herein have been designed and presented with the best knowledge and intent possible. This purchase in no way reflects a guarantee of success. Examples or results as described in this module are typical and should not be expected to provide the exact results nor should they be construed as promises for actual or future performance potential. You alone are responsible and accountable for your decisions, actions, and results in life, and by your purchase here you agree not to attempt to hold us liable for your decisions, actions or results, at any time, under any circumstance. There are NO refunds once this training course is purchased.

This information is for education purposes only and not to be considered as average or expected results, which will vary greatly based on your education level, systems, time, effort and many other factors solely within your control.

All materials covered and associated with this e-learning course are copyrighted. Any unauthorized reprint or use of these materials is prohibited. No part of any materials may be reproduced or transmitted in any form or by any means, electronic or mechanical, including photocopying, recording, or by any information storage and retrieval system without the express written permission of Dr. Linda J. Burrs and/or Step Up To Success LLC. Please contact Dr. Linda Burrs at Admin@DrBurrs.com.

CONTENTS

I   Welcome and Introduction   1

II   Pre-Course Instructions   5

ONE   Module 1 Discussion - The Journey Begins   7

TWO   Module 2 Discussion - Owning Your Purpose   19

THREE   Module 3 Discussion - Living Your Purpose   31

FOUR   Putting It All Together - The Plan   39

FIVE   Summary and Final Thoughts   45

I

WELCOME AND INTRODUCTION

I am Dr. Linda Burrs and am the President and Principal Consultant of the Step Up to Success Consulting firm, home of Second Generation diversity training. My firm focuses on leadership and organizational strategies. For more than 30 years, my purpose has been to bring my rich, fun, and dynamic approach to the corporate and professional training and executive coaching arena. The breadth of my experience crosses all walks of social and organizational life including law firms, law enforcement agencies, health care, and financial organizations including educators, business professionals, leadership groups, government entities, and non-profit groups.

I am excited you are taking this course to support you in your journey into self-discovery. You may find the process to be messy, comfortable and challenging. BUT, self-discovery can also be amazing, enlightening, and one of the most engaging experiences you can take yourself through. So, sit back, relax, and enjoy the journey. Let's get started.

Levoy (1998) said, "We must be willing to get shaken up, to submit ourselves to the dark blossoming of chaos in order to reap the blessings of growth" (p.8). Your "shaking up" can begin with this e-learning course designed just for you.

This course is about *living IN purpose*. When you live IN purpose, the guiding principles for you are love, passion, and wisdom. Wisdom comes from knowing you are doing what you were born to do and when you clearly understand your purpose, you begin to engage life in ways that are profound yet meaningful and transformational for yourself and others.

Purpose is like an energetic allure. You may not be able to explain a calling, but Ikigai draws you toward it to fulfill your life's intended mission. Deep in your heart lies an ember that is simmering. Not a hot feverish burn, but a persistent glow that stays alive in the promise that one day, you would find your way through the tangles of life to live your true purpose. Use this course to feed that soft glowing ember the oxygen of commitment and passion to bring forth the promise of Ikigai in your spirit.

There is never an expiration date on a dream. Sankofa is an African word from the Akan tribe in Ghana which translates to "it is not taboo to fetch what is at risk of being left behind." (www.Berea.edu). In other words, it is ok to go back and grab what you may have left behind. I am repeating this important point: **It is ok and not too late to go back and get what you left behind.** This course requires you to go deeper into exploring your life experiences to find the treasure of your purpose. Reach back and get "it.' As long as you are breathing, it is not too late.

There are always signs along the way that attempt to guide, direct, and show us the path. For whatever reason, purpose eludes some of us until we are ready to "see" it. Sometimes purpose walks into your life and sometimes it takes a while to figure out. Purpose can follow us unnoticed throughout our lives until in a single right moment, when you know something must change and that triggers you to know, now is the time.

Over the past 30 years, I have spent much of my career coaching others into their potential. For some, it meant moving on from a job that caused stress and painful experiences or sometimes they got into work no one but they thought was possible. I want to help you figure out what you really want to do, how to do it, and what it means to live IN your purpose.

It does not matter when you begin your journey. Some have known all their life what they were destined to do; they are the fortunate ones. Others figure it out in their 30's, 40's, 50's, and even into their 60's, before it all comes together. Many have to look for their purpose, or sometimes, your purpose finds you. So, let's get started.

II

PRE-COURSE INSTRUCTIONS

I am excited you have taken this step to make an important difference in your life beginning right now. I am glad you are here.

To get the most out of this course, keep the following in mind:

- As a self-paced course, go as fast or as slow as needed to understand and process the information you are learning about yourself.

- Be gentle with yourself. You may be making discoveries that exhilarate you or may cause some discomfort. Trust the process. Stay in the present and remain focused on your goal of living in your purpose.

- Be honest with yourself. Own your past and present successes and failures. You may feel you are being asked a lot of questions, some of which you may not understand the intent behind, so again, I ask you to trust the process. Most life changes begin with a change in how you think. Ralph Waldo Emerson suggested, "The mind, once stretched ... never returns to its original dimensions."

- Open your mind to possibilities. Let go of any need to control outcomes. Experience what it means to "go with the flow". Stay open.

- Do not be afraid to ask for help or to engage in discussions to share your thoughts. You are not alone. Develop healthy relationships with your support system.

- Learn from your frustrations, your challenges, and trust what experience has taught you (learning agility). Use what you are experiencing now to get to the next level of personal discovery.

- Everyone is born with a purpose. That said, do not expect this training course to instruct you in a step-by-step process. Purpose is found at the core of your being. This course helps bring awareness into your calling by taking you through an exploration of self-discovery. You are then presented with options of how to engage your purpose through the choices you make.

- When it comes to completing the exercises, it is very important to take the time to deeply think through your responses to each question. Challenge what you typically think, feel, and do. Your goal is to remove habitual ways of thinking that may have impeded your progress.

- You will be stretching your mind to new dimensions in order to think, feel, and make changes in how you see yourself. When you engage in multiple layers of learning, you can clear out old patterns of thinking that may have gotten in the way of you seeking and fulfilling your purpose. Stay focused, hopeful, and positive as you respond to the questions and work through the exercises.

ONE

MODULE 1 DISCUSSION - THE JOURNEY BEGINS

Conceptually, Ikigai (ee – key – guy) symbolizes finding one's purpose in life. Specifically, Ikigai means "reason for being". When you discover what truly lights your flame of passion, you can own your journey and live a purpose-driven life with confidence, fearlessness, and great joy, knowing you are doing what you believe you were born to do.

The last couple of years have left many feeling lost and questioning if they should begin a new career. If some of you began to look for answers to the question: Is this all there is? You are not alone. It does not matter if you are younger or older. Many have gone through life feeling there is something greater and more significant they could be doing. Millions of employees have left the workforce for various reasons, mostly because they've become fed up with miserable working conditions, inadequate pay, and poor treatment. If this is an example of what you have experienced, the question you could be asking yourself is: "what am I doing to discover my true purpose so I can transition to doing what brings me genuine joy, satisfaction, and passion into my life?"

Thought-starter: What choice can you make every day that will keep your passion for your calling "top of mind"? As you answer this and other thought-provoking questions during this training, you will be setting an intention to find the satisfaction and joy that comes from living in your purpose.

Many people feel like they have to live with regrets. Regrets for having worked so much at the expense of time spent with family and loved ones, in a job they may not have enjoyed. In spite of the challenges you faced, you have had a successful life and made a good living, yet, you feel something is missing in your life. Other regrets can include not living up to your potential. You wanted or meant to do more but it never seemed like the right time to continue your education or certification program to make yourself more marketable for the job you really wanted. Regardless of why you may be where you are now, it is not a life sentence. Your Ikigai is never out of reach. You can make the choice at any time to change your life's path and discover what you were born to do. It's time to make your life what you really truly want it to be.

Then, there are those who knew what they really wanted to do but lacked the tools, inner strength, or courage to take the actions required to make the choices to live in their purpose. Right now, think about what brings you joy or what gets you excited. Are you worth living your life on your terms? Do you understand you have a right to live life satisfied that what you are doing is best for you? Living with regrets can only deepen one's heaviness from an unsatisfied life.

Think back to when you were younger:

- Were you less fearful?

- Did you take more risks?

- Were you able to challenge yourself in pursuit of a goal?

- Did you teach yourself a sport or how to do something you always wanted to do just out of a sheer will?

As you remember what your younger self longed to do, what was it that made you hopeful, gave you meaning, or brought you joy? Now ask yourself:

- What would your younger self tell you now about the choices you make on how to live your life in purpose?

- What would your adult self tell your younger self to prepare for adulthood and what to watch out for?

Emotional trappings are signs of incongruence between your inner desires and outer turmoil. The trappings that get us caught up will not go away. These trappings are always going to be there, egging you on that other things should have priority over everything else. Have you ever wanted something so bad, you found a way to get it? When you use your grit and determination, the trappings loosen their grip on you and life finds a way.

Some trappings might include:

- The trappings of shame

- The trappings of guilt or of living life based on what other people think

- The trappings of disappointment from others

If you are able to see possibilities for change in your life in this moment, then carpe diem. Your journey has begun. Seize the day. The exercises that follow are designed to take you deeper into self-awareness to help you discover more about who you are and what you may have forgotten about who you wanted to be and what you wanted to do.

Exercise 1 for Module 1

As you go through this course, be aware of your mind's attempt to organize your thoughts while in creative thinking mode. Be open and accepting of yourself just as you are. You do not have to control your thoughts. You do not have to please anyone but yourself. Just let all your thoughts flow without restrictions. Write them all down. There are gems in the flow. You may sort them once you are done getting all your thoughts recorded.

Why does answering these questions matter? Because answering these questions can encourage you to engage in breakthrough thinking to initiate higher-order thinking (metacognition which is thinking about your thinking).

How do you start in this type of thinking?

- First, recognize the confines of your thinking and how it limits how you see yourself. Limited thinking shuts off your ability to see possibilities and will have you believe your purpose is not possible or realistic. Overcoming the restrictions of this type of thinking by understanding can illuminate your true Ikigai and bring it into focus. The light is your purpose; when recognized, it can light up your life with peace, joy, and happiness.

- Second, look for patterns in your recorded or written thoughts. What do you see? Write down the pattern you recognize in your thinking (i.e., motivating others, helping people heal, artworking with your hands (i.e., mechanical, technician, carpenter), working with numbers or shapes and forms (i.e., accountant, attorney, seamstress).

- Third, keep in mind your ego will, at times, try to work against you. The ego seems to like keeping things the same, but your soul knows better. Take some time to re- assure the ego. The ego wants to protect you from disappointment, pain, failure so it creates an identity for you. That identity is rigid in its thoughts, beliefs, and behaviors. Anything that does not fit the created identity, the ego will reject. Reassuring the ego you recognize its role as protector of who it thinks you are, lessens the resistance of the ego to interfere with the changes you intend to make.

- Fourth, take advantage of the powerful influence of intention. You give power to your purpose by setting intentions. Never forget you are the co-creator of your dreams. Visualize what you want, speak it, and then be confident that whatever the outcome it can be for your greatest good and highest joy. Know that living your purpose is already available to you. It is important to remain hopeful and focused. The powerful combination of focus and intention has the potential to create the desires of your heart.

- Finally, realize that when you have a clear idea of your purpose and the intention to prepare yourself to receive and use your gifts, the door of possibilities begins to attract what you need to get what you want.

- As you set your purpose with intention, speak it aloud with the specificity you want and feel deep inside you. Be clear on what you want. Then see, feel, and experience what it might be like to get what you want. Commit to doing what you need to do to reach your intended purpose. If you need to go back to school to get a certificate or degree include that as part of your intentions. Share your expectations with those who support you, or, if you don't have a support network yet, speak it to the wind. Whatever you choose, your intention sets up a series of experiences to help bring your Ikigai into your reality in its own time.

- Pay attention to the signals and messages that are guiding you on your journey. Don't be afraid to try new ideas and by all means, don't worry about what someone else might think of what you intend to accomplish.

NOTE: When you see a puzzle piece with the question mark throughout this course, recognize these markers as prompts to respond to each question.

Now, begin by responding to the following questions:

Who am I? (Tell yourself about yourself)

What parts of yourself did you abandon years ago?

Why am I here? (Not why here in this present moment but why am I here on this earth?)

What do others often say you are very good at doing?

What do people constantly compliment you on?

What is your current reality? Do your dreams have more power than doubts?

What is it that you feel especially proud of?

What gifts do you have that help you serve others?

In what ways have you been recognized by others that have really touched you?

What have you rejected about yourself?

What makes you uncomfortable? Where do these uncomfortable feelings originate?

What is your greatest fear?

What is hardest to embrace about yourself? Why?

What is in the "Bag You Drag"? What are you holding onto that is getting in your way of progressing in the way you want?

Identify what you want by first acknowledging what you don't want. What needs to change for you right now? Remember, you cannot change what you can't or don't acknowledge.

Focus on what you intend to change and the positive energy that feeling generates.

NOTES:

Exercise 2 for Module 1

Using the responses to your questions in Exercise #1, the patterns from your thoughts, and how you see your future, write down what you believe your true purpose in life may be. Include why you believe this to be true. You don't have to be 100% certain right now. You are free to change what you think is best for you later in the course.

 What is the central theme of my life, my soul's heart code?

If I could create one new thing for myself, what would that new thing be?

If I could change one thing for myself, what would that one thing be?

If I could add one thing to my life, what would that one thing be?

What would my younger self want me to be doing?

What belief systems do I think I need to change since they no longer serve me or work in my best interest?

What strategies will I use to make these changes real and lasting? In other words, what is my call to action?

If I get off-track, how will I get myself back in the flow?

NOTE: You can spend your time judging yourself or loving yourself. Which do you think has more value?

What gifts do I have that will help me help others?

How will I use my energy and effort to explore all the possibilities available to me now, that can help me live positively in my purpose?

In what ways have I been recognized by others that have really touched me?

What have I rejected about myself?

What makes me uncomfortable?

What is my greatest fear?

What do I find hardest to embrace in myself? Why?

Remember, you cannot change what you cannot acknowledge. Focus on what you intend to change and the positive energy embracing that change generates for you.

Ikigai:
Module Two
Owning Your Purpose

TWO

MODULE 2 DISCUSSION - OWNING YOUR PURPOSE

In the Chichewa (chuh•chay•wuh) language, the word **umwini** means ownership. To own is to have, hold, or possess. When you own your purpose, you have a settled and resolve determination to pursue your calling. In this module, the discussion turns from exploring options to developing strategies you may use to own and live with your Ikigai. As you consider what you want to do next, think through what you may need to add or delete from the experiences you are now engaged in. Everyone is different and every individual will approach owning their purpose in a way that is best for them. What is presented here are suggestions and ideas that have worked for others and could work for you. Before you start answering questions, consider the following information.

Metacognition (thinking about your thinking)

In this module, the questions you are being asked have the goal of helping you get beyond how you traditionally approach solving complex issues. These questions invite you to delve deeper into your thinking by recognizing patterns of behavior that may be getting in the way of you totally owning your purpose. In order to truly change, you have to change how you see yourself and how you think about who you are and what you truly want to do.

Thought-starter: What do I need to add to my life now, that prepares me to own my purpose? Remember, what you think, influences what you do.

Deep inside of your brain are memories that hold what you came to this earth to do. The calling is still there but it may be buried so deep it is hard to recognize or even see. Alternatively, you may know what you have been called to do but made choices that took you down a road that diverged from your true calling. Either way, it is time to take a long hard look at where you really want to be. Now is the time to examine your thinking (cognitive) processes. Not all of them…just the ones relevant to your calling.

How do you arrive at conclusions—quickly or do you take your time? If you know you are quick to rush to conclusions, you may want to slow down the process a bit by reflecting on these three questions.

- What don't I know?

- What information about this situation don't I have?

- What else could be true?

When you slow down enough to contemplate other options or alternatives, you give yourself an opportunity to learn more information about what you believe to be true. Are there words, expressions, or experiences that tend to trigger immediate responses? If so, develop the habit of thinking about your thinking. This is called metacognition. Take the time to collect enough information to be able to frame the best response possible to each question. This includes understanding what triggers you.

Triggers are responses to anything that causes an emotional reaction from you. These emotional reactions can cause you to become reactive, overwhelmed, or even elicit a distress response. Why is this important to know? Because many times when an individual attempts to change, triggers show up as resistance to your best efforts.

The mind has been conditioned to stay the same. The brain likes consistency. In order to feel comfortable with change, new neural networks need to be built. That means overcoming the resistance reflected in your triggers. When triggered, it is important to respond differently than how you typically respond.

It is important to sift through surface thinking to understand what is influencing the belief systems about yourself. Thoughts, like words, carry weight and significant influence. You are who you believe yourself to be. When you resolve to live in your purpose, you have started to create a new neural network that can continue to grow the more you engage in thinking that supports your goal. The new network can help support your efforts to change. Go back and "get" what you left behind…its ok. Your true purpose is waiting for you.

Adding and deleting

What you may have come to understand is that our thoughts create beliefs and what you believe you deserve, is often what you get.

Thought-starter: What do you think influences your actions? Here is something I have found helpful to do. Sift through surface thinking to understand what is influencing your belief systems and thus your present thinking. Thoughts and words are energetic and will influence every aspect of your life. Can you see how action follows thought?

There are beliefs and perceptions that should be deleted or added to the patterns in how you think. What are some things you want to delete from your brain's network?

- Worry ("Worrying is using your imagination to create something you don't want" (Esther Hicks).

- Emotional contagion is the transfer of emotional energies from one person to another. Emotional contagion can be a social construct that impacts your beliefs about yourself and what you are or are not capable of doing. Pay attention to your thinking. Can you remember where that way of thinking originated?

- Internal and external objections from others (and yourself). Be prepared to manage your own objections and the external objections from others. It can be helpful to develop a personal meme for yourself that is meaningful, persuasive, and intentional in its ability to keep you on track when life or others get in your way (i.e., face your fear(s) and do it anyway).

There are also ways of thinking and feeling that you may want to add to your network of how you think. Some of them are confidence, compassion, and patience (what else do you want to add?). Being open to others' ideas, perspectives, and beliefs help you to be open to your own. It can help you better understand what you may want to change.

When feeling uncertain or fearful, practice self-care:

- Go for a walk, swim, or bicycle (or other exercise)

- Sit in the sunshine

- Meditate or listen to music you love

- Dance

- Flush your system – drink water

- Practice breathing exercises that help you relax

- Use color and/or aroma therapies

Sometimes making a public statement can help you gain a stronger level of commitment. Some experts say public statements are good as the statements made to others can help hold you accountable. Other experts say it is not helpful and only causes additional stress. You get to decide what works best for you. Publicly stating an intention can generally hold you accountable for what you say and do. It is important to share your intentions with your team of supporters. Ask for their help to keep you dedicated and on track. Most important is the need to remain focused and energized about your goals.

- Energize yourself and your purpose every day (read, discuss, do something that strengthens your resolve and helps you get closer to your calling).

- Be grateful for the opportunity to do what you love

- Commit to being the change that will make a difference for others

- Look for ways to increase your knowledge about your purpose

- Improve your skills with practice (volunteer, offer gifts of support, share experiences)

- Journal your journey ("At the end of the pen is a friend" that never criticizes or condemns)

- Electronic notes

- Video

- Write a blog

Exercise 1 for Module 2

Please answer each question with careful and deep reflection. Reflect on how you respond to your triggers.

 What are my triggers?

How do I generally respond to these triggers?

Can my typical response to my triggers help or hurt my efforts to own my purpose? Why or why not?

What do I need to change about my triggers?

What obstacles are in my path right now? How can these potential stumbling blocks be removed?

What is my belief system about how I prefer to live my life?

How do I know when I need to change course? How did I know it was time to act?

How will I go about changing?

What is the central theme of my life (my soul's heart code)?

If I could change one thing about myself, what would that one thing be?

What would my younger self want me to be doing?

What belief systems do I intend to change since they no longer serve me or my best interest because they have hindered me in the past?

What strategies will I use to make these changes real and lasting? In other words, What is my call to action?

How will I get myself back in the flow if I get off track?

NOTE: You can spend your time judging or loving yourself. Which do you think has more value?

You could try affirmations, meditations or prayer, or deep breathing exercises to stay grounded (connected and stable).

NOTE: It is important to imprint your purpose into your heart, mind, and soul. Repetition creates new mental networks in the brain thereby creating new or updated beliefs.

Exercise 2 for Module 2

First, write down what you see you need to add to and what you need to delete from your life

 +   Add

-   Delete

Second, write out what you are ready and prepared to share with the world about who you are.

(A 20-second elevator pitch)

Third, what will you do every day as preparation to live in your purpose? (i.e., what do you need to add/delete, meditate, pray, set the intentions to expect success, journal your successes and what you need to improve)

THREE

MODULE 3 DISCUSSION - LIVING YOUR PURPOSE

Now that you have worked through the questions and more importantly, your responses, you may have a clearer perspective or memory of what your calling is.

You may also have uncovered some gifts that make you unique. Now you can see what brings you genuine joy; what connects you with your emotions and passions deeply and profoundly. As you embrace this new reality, it can feel meaningful and exciting, and most importantly, you have a more realistic way of seeing your way through potential challenges to begin living life in your purpose.

So, how does one go about transitioning into this new reality?

Reframe – Acknowledge what you are going through and then do something different. Give the picture or image in your mind a new look. Can current behaviors help you get where you want to be? How do you know the path you are on is not the path forward?

Refocus – Adjust the lens on your reframe. Is it possible that what you are experiencing is necessary to your journey?

Refresh – This is a reference to some old technology, but refreshing is like pressing the F5 button or swiping down a screen to get new information. While you are "refreshing", holding space (which means to be empathetic and understanding) with yourself can give you a mental safe place to adjust and get back on track.

Review and evaluate – This is like proofreading a paper before submitting it for a final critique. If you find yourself off track, take a look at what you intended to do to see if you have left something out. Fear comes when there is uncertainty. Is this what you want to do? If the answer is yes, move ahead. If the answer is no, what has changed since you chose to take this course?

- Are you ready to move ahead?

- Do you recognize what may be driving you in an opposite direction?

- Do you have the tools to make the adjustments you need to move forward? If not, what tools do you need and how will you get them? Add the tools you need to your list of goals.

- What are you prepared to commit to in this moment?

Readjust – It is possible to readjust by re-releasing old patterns that hold you back or that feed your fears. Try settling into the idea that the unknown could be a blessing.

- This adjustment can allow you to create space for even greater possibilities in your life. It is important to trust that what is for you will always be for you and that no one, but you, can take it away.

- "Finding your life's meaning or purpose is an essential motivation of every person" (Murray 1999). Sometimes the "what you really want" will come in a "roundabout way". If you have a low tolerance for uncertainty, focus on this thought: deep uncertainty is often a result of perfectionism. Let go of the need to be "perfect". Work towards accepting uncertainties and see them as moments for positive change. The world is looking for your best and your best is often imperfect.

- Know that what you have been looking for has been looking for you and waiting for you to let go of what is not serving or helping you.

- Fear takes up a lot of space. When you let go of what no longer serves your best interests, you have made room to soar into your purpose. When you let go of your fears, you make space for the miraculous to move in. You have created the opportunity to live in your purpose. Having hope is the only thing that is stronger than fear.

- Deal with limiting beliefs. These are the self-imposed beliefs you have about yourself that cause you to place restrictions on what you think and feel and consequently what you do. Work through them using the following suggestions:

- Please know that fears do not belong in your dreams.

- Do not say NO before you explore YES.

- Confront negative attitudes that may have been exposed during this course.

- Face your fears and doubts.

- Recognize the power of intention. Speak your intentions into existence.

- Honor yourself every day. Do at least one meaningful and self-honoring activity every day (hot salt bath, quiet time, time with friends, a relaxing evening with loved ones, enjoy a favorite meal or book).

- Reject limiting beliefs by utilizing positive turnaround statements which are generally the opposite of the limiting belief (i.e., Turn around the limiting belief of, "I am afraid this may not work" into "I have confidence I am going to do this" or "I want to do this. I can do this. I have to do this. I WILL do this.").

- Use positive statements to change the energy of your belief from a negative into a positive statement that feeds your expectation in the direction you want it to go. Remember…anything you say after "I am" sets an intention for what you want to happen. "I am successful." "I am open to possibilities." "I am creating my future."

After you have completed The Plan—putting it all together, you will have in your possession a specific plan designed by you, for you.

Exercise 1 for Module 3

Living in your purpose requires a life theme that you believe can guide you during times of challenge and stress. Create your personal meme which is an idea or behavioral expression that defines what you want others to know about you. A helpful resource is http://www.quickmeme.com/.

James Hillman (1996) said your purpose is like a magnet to your soul and that following the guidance of your soul takes a leap of faith. When you are ready to take that leap of faith, here are some things you can do:

Shift your commitment into high gear

Designing your purpose meme:

 Come up with a code-word or phrase to bring yourself back into purpose when you feel yourself slip or feel like you can't do this. Write out your code word or phrase.

Having a code word can give you an ability to see beyond where you are now by encouraging you to pick up new and fresh ideas that add to your body of wisdom. A life theme can also help keep your ego in check. Don't forget, your ego likes to keep things the same.

Learn breathing exercises to help you become and remain grounded (attentive and stable).

Use affirmations and meditations (guided or not) to help you stay focused. Write out your personal affirmation and/or select a meditation.

Imprint your purpose into your heart, mind, and soul. Repetition creates new systems in the brain thereby creating new beliefs. Write out your purpose.

Exercise 2 for Module 3

Using what you learned from Modules 1, 2, and 3, put together your plan for living in your purpose.

 When do I expect to begin the changes? (You want to have a timeframe plan to help you stay on course) (immediately, in a month?)

What resources do I need to have in place?

(training, education, certificate, apprenticeship)

How will I acquire these resources?

How will I market any changes I intend to make in my life?

What type of help do I think I will need? (mentorship, financial, organization, time management, strategic planning). How will you get this help?

- Surround yourself with love

  ✓ Self-love

  ✓ Others who love you and consistently support your dream

- Remember, fear can be suffocating

  ✓ What strategies will you use to deal with fear or any emotion that may negatively affect your plans?

  ✓ Help someone else succeed

    o One of the best ways to live in your purpose is to help someone else succeed

    o Helping others keeps you remain focused on your growth so you are able to help others

    o Helping others is positive energy that will come back to you as move toward the success you are seeking

  ✓ Creates a "line of sight" where your life's purpose is always at the "top" of your mind

  ✓ Gives you an ability to see beyond where you are now by encouraging you to pick up new and fresh ideas that add to your body of wisdom

FOUR

PUTTING IT ALL TOGETHER - THE PLAN

What is the most important thing you learned about yourself?

Who are you? What makes you unique? What energizes or gets you excited? What brings you joy? What are you passionate about?

What are your gifts, talents, or unique abilities?

What do other people regularly comment on or speak positively about you?

Clearly define your purpose and why you believe this to be true for you?

What do you need to add or delete to achieve this goal? List everything to which you can commit, to make your Ikigai a reality in your life.

What are your triggers? How will you manage them? What will you do to overcome the negative impact of your triggers?

Earlier you were asked to design a personal meme that reminds you of who you are and what you intend to do. What is your personal meme? Explain the significance of your meme to you personally? How will you use this meme to help you stay focused?

What is your personal public statement (your 30-second commercial statement about who you are)?

What will you do with fear or a loss of focus?

How will you journal your journey?

What resources, training, and support do you need to keep moving forward in your plan?

Who will you ask to join your support network? What and how do you want support from each person or resource?

How will you measure your progress toward your Ikigai? What are the important milestones you will monitor and track?

How do you plan to stay on track?

How will you know you have reached your goal?

What will you do to celebrate your achievement?

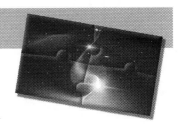

FIVE

SUMMARY AND FINAL THOUGHTS

This is your dream, no one else's. You may feel you are finally on the right path to living in purpose with your life. Now that you are here, let's briefly discuss ways to deal with fear. Fear, is the root cause for most, if not all, of the negative emotional disruptions in life. If you are paying attention, you may be able to see how fear can insert itself through negative emotions, especially frustration, jealousy, exhaustion, anger, or any number of ways we can be emotionally overwhelmed. You cannot be in the flow of positivity and fear at the same time. Pay attention to your thoughts and "see" them. You must choose what you will focus on.

What can you do when fear increases your stress in unhealthy ways? It is important to acknowledge, feel, and then release the fear. Fear, like courage, or any other emotion, is energetic. Suppressing emotions is not healthy. If you try to act as if it is not there, it can worsen. Holding space (being empathetic and understanding) with yourself as you make this adjustment will go a long way toward getting yourself in a better place emotionally.

Holding space and focusing on wrapping yourself in the positive energy of courage is one way to help you through what is happening. Sound a little far-fetched? Try this:

- Close your eyes and imagine something you have done in the past that required you to be courageous (take a new job, speak up for yourself or for someone else, decide to stop being undervalued, public speaking). How did it feel? Where in your body did you feel the emotion? Did your heart rate speed up or slow down? Did that decision make you feel better or worse about what you were doing? Describe how you were feeling when it was all over.

Use this experience to remember what courage felt like and where in your body you felt it. Repeat this process whenever you begin to feel fearful, frustrated, or angry. Take a minute to get in a place of comfort and breathe into the space where you feel the emotion the most. Allow yourself to feel better.

Resources that may be helpful to you on your journey:

https://youtu.be/7xmGi9UzVIY

https://youtu.be/zya9IeRzfwE

https://youtu.be/a7q_vACVwq0

Final thoughts

Oprah Winfrey, American Television Host and Publisher has been credited with saying, "There is no greater gift you can give or receive than to honor your calling. It's why you were born. And how you become most truly alive" (year unknown). When you put your whole self into the discovery process; your mind, body, and spirit will support your mission to create what you need. By using your whole self, you can metaphorically cloak yourself in the "fabric of creation" and offer gratitude, love, and compassion to every- thing you think, feel, and everything you do.

During this course you have asked yourself "Who am I?", "Why am I here?", and "What will I do?" These are all especially important questions for you to be able to answer. Remember the two words, **I AM**, before anything else you say becomes a self-fulfilling prophecy. Your thoughts, words, and actions matter.

Avoid looking for problems. Trust your heart, it will never lie to you. It will take courage, determination, pervasive self-love, and respect for yourself to make this happen. Persistence will be your best friend, wisdom your guiding light, and a deep and unyielding promise to stay on the path of discovery. This can strengthen hope and trust that you will find, own, and live in your purpose. Remember, above all else, continue to embrace your Ikigai. In it you will find the courage, confidence, and commitment to be the best version of yourself every single day.

As you continue to build your support network, don't be afraid to ask for help. It will also be important to network with those who work in the field of your calling. Get creative. Use Zoom or Microsoft Teams if you cannot meet in person. Use social media to start support groups and discussions.

Beliefs are merely thoughts that you repeatedly think. If that belief is getting in the way of recognizing and engaging your purpose, stop repeating that thinking pattern. Those are the thoughts you don't want if your goal is to change. Having a "thought buddy" system to bounce ideas off can lead to valuable relationships and support. Consider hiring a credible executive or business coach if you are able. In every instance, be kind, patient, and loving with yourself.

Give thanks for the peace that comes with finding, owning, and living in your purpose. Please remember, you can go back and get what you left and promise yourself to stay fiercely committed, passionate, and engaged in the process. Change your belief systems and you can change your life. Only you can choose to make these changes. It is all up to you. **"It matters not how strait the gate, how charged with punishments the scroll, I am the master of my fate, I am the captain of my soul"** (quoted from the poem Invictus by Willam Ernest Henley). Watch, as beautiful things happen when you stay in the flow. I wish you all the best on your exciting journey.

Dr. B

NOTES:

_____

_____

_____

_____

_____

_____

_____

_____

_____

_____

_____

_____

_____

_____

_____

_____

_____

_____

_____

_____

NOTES:

References

Hillman, James. 1996. The soul's code: in search of character and calling. New York: Random House.

Levoy, Gregg. (1998). Callings: finding and following an authentic life. New York: Random House of Canada. Henley, William Ernest. (1875). https://worldview. unc.edu/news-article/invictus/#:~:text=Nelson%20Man-   dela%2C%20the%20 anti%2Dapartheid,1875%20by%20William%20Ernest%20Henley. https://en.opentran.net/chichewa-english/umwini.html

https://www.goodreads.com/quotes/9937629-worrying-is-using-your-imagination-to-create-something- you-don-t

https://www.berea.edu/cgwc/the-power-of-sankofa/#:~:text=The%20literal%20 translation%20of%20 the,look%2C%20seek%20and%20take).

https://www.oprah.com/spirit/oprah-on-finding-your-calling-what-i-know-for-sure#:~:text=What%20 I%20know%20for%20sure%3A%20There%20is%20no%20 greater%20gift,you%20become%20most%20 truly%20alive.

Printed in the United States
by Baker & Taylor Publisher Services